What I wish I knew before starting an online business:

50 Tips For Starting an Online Business

Shonda Miles

Other books by Author

10 Ways to Write an Ebook every 10 days

101 Success Questions

Remote Medical Coding Jobs

How to break into Medical Coding

Tips for Staring an Online Business

How to Love Your Spouse again

How to Double Your Income in 12 Months or less

50 Tips to Jumpstart Your Success

50 Streams of Income

How to Get the Job You Want

I am

I am for girls

I am for Teens

I am for boys

Why am I fat

Girl Power

30 Days to Being a Better Christian

Contents

For more information on Shonda Miles, go to www.shondamiles.com. Shonda Miles offers a range of Products and Services including Multiple Streams of Income-how to make money while you sleep and How to make an extra $100,000 this year.

To my husband,
Thank You for Your Support

"Take up one idea and act on it. Make that one idea your life. Think of it, dream of it, and live on that idea. Let the brain, muscles, nerves, and every part of your body be full of that idea and leave all other ideas along. This is the way to success."

"Allow yourself to dream and fantasize about your ideal life; what it would look like, and what it would feel like. Then do something every day to make it a reality!" Brian Tracy

Tip 1

Buyers online don't care who you are as long as you can help them solve their problems.

If you have what people want, they will buy it.

There are ready and willing buyers you just need to find them.

People are buying stuff every day, just look around you.

Look around you at the addicts of the world: people who love fly fishing, golf, scrap booking, or football teams they will buy anything related to that team, golf, or scrap booking. They just don't buy one thing but everything they can find on that subject.

I am not sure who said this but "It is much better to launch your product even if it's not perfect and start to make money with it."

Tip 2

Don't take advice from anyone who hasn't been successful.

"We all have people around us who mean well with their advice but in reality they are not that helpful and not that successful themselves. It is very dangerous to take advice from them."

Protect your business idea from naysayers and negative people. Cultivate your ideas by doing research and by asking certain people for input. Continue to nurture the idea. Ask someone who has some experience in the field or who is an expert. You can even ask someone who you trust.

The reason why I started an online business is because I got tired of, If I didn't show up to work I didn't get paid. "If you do what you've always done you will continue to get what you've always gotten." Decide to do something different.

Tip 3

One thing to remember is, it doesn't happen overnight. It could take 2 years, just don't give up. If you're serious about having an online business, don't give up. You very well could with some hard work get your business going and earning the money you desire online right away.

Success takes time. We have to put in the effort. Be patient.

According to Jay Lipe, "The first three times you promote something; you're really just creating awareness. The next twelve times you're reinforcing the awareness and beginning to uncover a need. And only by the twentieth time, will your prospect take action"

You need as many touch points as possible. What I mean by this is a customer doesn't buy from you usually the first time. A customer has to see you or your Business Name and or Service over and over before they stand up and take notice.

You can use your free offer or free eBook, YouTube videos, podcasts, newsletters, blogging, social media, daily email to get these touchpoints. It's important to know how to build relationships. You want to be able to help people by adding value.

You have to give before you get.

Tip 4

Know your target market. What is your customer? How old are they? What do they do for a living? How much money do they make?

Is your best customer male or female? What are there hobbies? Where do they hang out? What do they read?

What are their most pressing need right now? What are their problems? What are their pain points? What is your solution? Speak to them in their language.

Get a picture in your mind of who that is. If you see a picture somewhere and you think, "Okay, this is who my target market looks like or this is the type of person that I would target."

Then you can write your copy to that person. You can write your books to that person, talking directly to that one person. It will just keep you focused where you're not talking to 10 different markets in one sales letter.

Of course you can have 10 different markets, that is not what I am saying. What I am saying is for each market, then you should do this.

Tip 5

It's necessary to have some type of referral system. You want to be able to, if someone buys your product or if someone signs up for a free webinar, you want to have some way that they can invite other people through social media or forward an email telling people about you or your freebie whether free ebook or webinar.

Tip 6

Online, I didn't realize how important it is, but it is so important to try to build a platform. You want to have people on your social media, your Facebook, your LinkedIn and your Twitter account.

You want people that are on your Pinterest if that's appealing for your target market, or Instagram. You can do this by making daily post and engaging with people. You can do this by offering valuable content. It can be automated through a Hootsuite. You can outsource this as well to someone at Upwork, Fiverr, Guru. You can get a VA to do this rather inexpensively.

It is necessary to have some type of platform where you can go to them and cultivate relationships. You can and advertise your events, webinars, or tele-seminars. Webinars and teleseminars are great ways for people to get to know you. Periscope, Blab, Facebook Live gives people the more intimate relationship you would get in person.

The important thing is to have an editorial calendar. You should have 80% content and 20% promotion.

If you have a platform, you'll be able to sell your products or services to them and literally have cash in the bank. Maybe you have a new book that's coming out. You can advertise it or let people know you've got a new book coming out. Include your tribe or even potential customers in the design process with cover choices maybe with title, subtitle choices or giving them excerpts from the book. They will feel like they were a part of your project by giving their input.

Build a tribe. You want to build a tribe and you'll start noticing how different businesses are starting to build tribes and they have their own name. They call them "something nation." This is important. It gives people a sense of community.

Tip 7

Tony Robbins says "If you want to be successful, find someone who has achieved the results you want and copy what they do and you'll achieve the same results."

Learn all you can from those who have done it. This is so important. You can learn so much from somebody who's been there and done it.

Buy your competitor's products. See what you can improve upon. Look at reviews or feedback from customers. Think about what you like or dislike about the product.

Get a mentor. They can literally shave years off the learning curve. They will be their worth their weight in gold.

Hire a Coach. If you decide to hire a coach, it's certainly worth the money, it will save you a lot of time and years wasted. Coaching-There are all types of Coaches. There are Health coaches, Business coaches, Marketing Coaches, Relationship Coaches, Career Coaches, Spiritual Coaches, Sales Coaches, Executive Coaches, Life Coaches and on and on. "Professional Coaching brings many wonderful benefits, fresh perspectives on personal challenges interpersonal effectiveness and increased confidence. And the list does not end there." ICF

"Coaching benefits your clients by helping them identify the goals and dreams that will bring them real lasting happiness. It also helps them remove the obstacles, limitations and circumstances that are holding them back from those those dreams, and it shows them how to make their ideal life a reality." Mary Morrissey

A Coach usually has some type of training or certification. As of this writing there is no governing body for Coaches which means there are people getting a business license and calling themselves a coach with no formal training. If you want to be in business for a long time and really help people some type of training is needed. International Coaching Federation is popular for offering coaching certification. You can google the Coaching you are interested in and type training or certification behind it. Also Read Anyone can Coach by Sean Mize. You can coach people all over the world over the phone. In order to be a good coach you must be a good listener with good analytical skills. In Coaching Clues, Marian J Their says "A coach is not a business partner, therapist, buddy, or confidant. The coaching relationship is a negotiated partnership in which all parties must respect each other and remain committed to the boundaries of a professional relationship. Small changes can make a huge difference." A business coach (specializing in small business) can prove to be very beneficial. A business coach can often help you catapult your success (business) to next level in a short period of time. A business coach is often a sounding board, an accountability partner, a cheerleader someone committed to your success. A business coaches main goal is to help you to be successful. This happens because they provide expertise in areas you are struggling with. They often can help you figure out what is holding you back. They can suggest small incremental changes that can make a big difference.

You can learn a great deal from a mastermind group. A mastermind group is a group of like-minded people who help support each other.

They meet weekly or biweekly. They offer a fresh set of eyes to a situation.

Of course, consider buying products from people who have already been there and done that. There's no sense in re-inventing the wheel.

Tip 8

Read about business at least weekly. You want to learn as much as you can as fast as you can about Internet marketing and all facets of your business.

If you spend time learning and applying what you learn about Marketing, Copywriting, How to Scale a business, Social Media Marketing, virality and building good relationships, you will be ahead of your competitors.

Tip 9

Don't waste time. People with online businesses do more busy work than actually work that produces results.

So stop surfing the internet and I know I'm guilty of this, and so I'm talking to myself as well. Stop checking email and get back to work. Pay attention to where your time goes.

Tip 10

Bradley J Sugars raises an interesting question could you wake up in the morning and call your office and say to whoever answered you all hold the fort. I am taking of the next three months.

"Would there be mass panic or would things run smoothly while you were gone. Would you be so worried about your business that you couldn't take three months off? Well if you would like to get into a position to take three months off and be free from worry listen to the following very closely."

In order to take your business to the next level the owner has to delegate standard business activities, using systems. This will free the owner up to work on growing the business. Without systems the owner will continue to be overworked, putting out fires all day never getting anything done. Not only that but things will be chaotic, out of order.

Systems are easy to understand.

Systems are repeatable.

In *The 51 Fatal Business Errors*, Jim Muehlhausen explains "Your business will not grow meaningfully with you doing the work. If you are doing the day to day, you are the bottle."

What is a system and how can it help my business

Systems are a written document of step-by-step procedures of how to do something. Systems are vital to every business whether it is a solopreneur or a 1,000 employee company. Systems create consistency and reliability for the customer. It saves time and resources. There are a multitude of systems that can be used in every business including hiring, follow up, customer service.

Apply systems to your business. This is really a big thing. If you want to ever walk away from your business, go on vacation and have your business run without you. As quick as you can you want to start writing down the things that you do in your business, especially those repetitive tasks.

You want to write all those things down, the way you do things, your process so that you can hire people for those jobs.

If you need to go on vacation or you want to be able to work on your business instead of in your business every single day, you want to have those systems in place where you can automate everything that you can, or be able to hire out those positions.

Having an online business takes work. It takes focus, but you have to make up your mind what is it you are trying to do? What are you trying to accomplish? You will have to work hard at least at first. A successful online business requires systems and automation. A successful online business owner is an internet marketer, and they're comfortable learning new things as things are changing so rapidly. Technology is used online often to decrease the time it takes to do something.

Creating systems helps you gain clarity and focus.

Creating systems puts the business owner in control. It takes the business owner from working in the business to working on the business.

Creating systems creates a turnkey business that runs without you.

"Success is not inherent in the act of franchising the business, but rather in the formula owners use in organizing and operating the business as a turnkey system. And the power of this franchise formula can be applied to any business anytime, anywhere to achieve maximum productivity and profitability."

Tip 11

Hire help as soon as you can. For example, a Virtual Assistant (VA). VAs can prove to be invaluable, especially helping with tasks that are repetitive.

What I found is just like with anything, there are good Virtual Assistants and not so good Virtual Assistants.

Virtual Freedom by Chris Ducker is a great book to read to help you learn more about how to use Virtual Assistants to grow your business. It will help you figure out how to hire VAs. I just advise to be careful hiring VAs - you want to be clear with your expectations.

You want to be clear with what it is that you're looking for, and what exactly you need help with, and what you want the VA to do.

You also want to make sure that you train the VA, and that you check and make sure that they're doing what they're supposed to do.

We probably all have nightmare stories, but this has been a nightmare for me at times. In certain instances, I've had a VA and it has proved to be a nightmare, but when it works it really works.

You might have to go through several VAs before you find one that works for you, but it's certainly worth it.

Tip 12

Be positive. Be confident. You will have rough days like we all do. If you work on a job you have times when you just have to keep yourself motivated.

You have to stay confident that things will work out like they are supposed to. Believe things will get better. Believe that your business will start to grow. Work your butt off doing the right things so it will.

You want to keep that positive, optimistic attitude. You just want to keep moving forward. You've got to believe in yourself and what you have to offer. You've got to believe that you can become a successful business owner.

Tip 13

Everyone is in the marketing business. Commit to marketing 1 day a week or 2 hours a day.

No matter what business you have, if you have a craft store or you are a Consultant or a social media marketer. If you have a dog website, you're in the marketing business.

There's no sense in having a good product if you don't market it. If you don't market your business, no one will know it exists. You want to make sure that you spend the time marketing your business at least weekly.

Tip 14

Do what you love. We get caught up in what's going to make money. What's going to make money? I hear this over and over again.

I believe this to be true -that if you do what you love, the money will come. It's hard to stay with a business just for the money when you're not making any money.

It's easy to do something that you love and then the money will start to come and then you'll be happier with the money, but you'll be happy while you're waiting.

You have a reason to stick with it, because you love it. Whereas, if you're just doing it for the money, when adversity comes or you fail or you make a mistake, then you're less likely to stay with it or it's harder to stay with it.

Don't do it for the money. It may be a long time until the money comes. When the money does come, you want to always reinvest some of your profits back into your business so that you can keep it growing, keeping it moving so that you can continue to market your business.

Tip 15

"A goal without a plan is just a wish." Antoine DeSaint Exupery

"Plans are nothing, planning is everything." Dwight D. Eisenhower

You need a plan. When I first started I just thought, "I'll start this business. I'm going to make money. I don't really have to have a plan," but a plan is essential.

You will definitely need an internet marketing plan and a social media marketing strategy. This is- How will people find you? Who is your target market? What is your marketing budget? How will you reach your target market? These things are so important.

Tip 16

You may need more than one website. This is more an advanced strategy. I don't want to get into this too much. I believe you get one site up and going, making money, profitable. Then you set up another one on a difference niche. You may be able to wait a while on this.

You find another niche that you're interested in, or you have one main website that's your name.

For example, mine is www.ShondaMiles.com. Then you have another site that's niche-based only. This will let you concentrate on another niche.

Tip 17

You need a sales funnel, up sell and down sell. This is, if you want to make any money, you want to know how to market your business, and you want to know how to sell.

A sales funnel is the way your customers or potential prospects come to you. At the top of the funnel you might have a free item, or a low-priced item.

Maybe the free item is a way to get people into your sales funnel. Then once they get into your sales funnel you might offer them right away a low-priced item between $19, $47 up to $97.

Then the next thing, you might offer something that's maybe $197. Then $497, or $597 or $997, then $1997, something like that. At every stage in the sales funnel, you should be offering them one stage up.

If you have– (I think I heard this from Sean Mize) 12 products or services in your sales funnel, then you can really play with this and try to up sell them. If they don't buy the up sell, you can down sell them. This is a great way to make money and be profitable.

Tip 18

You need more than one stream of income. If you have a coaching business, you want to do more than just coach clients.

You want to have some way to offer your customers information products, audio products, courses or membership site. You want to have books on Amazon Kindle, you want to have regular books on Amazon.

Perhaps you want to do real estate investing as well. Maybe you have some joint venture partners. You just want to have more than one stream of income.

Being in business can be brutal. Sometimes it can be feast or famine. Until you really learn how to run your business, you could have a lot of months where it is up and down.

Tip 19

Use webinars to grow your business. You can do a free trial through GotoWebinar.com. There are a lot of other Webinar Platforms such as Google Hangouts, Webinar Jam, Fuze or ClickWebinar.

You can use a Facebook ad where you offer a free webinar teaching your potential clients something they want to learn that really adds value.

Teach your customers good content. Then at the end, you can sell them on your service. If that's coaching or consulting, especially if you're just starting out.

You can offer coaching or a boot camp. You can do a tele-class. You can do e-courses. You can offer the free webinar and then at the end of the free webinar, you can offer your service.

Tip 20

You need to write interesting, valuable content, or be able to hire someone that can. This takes some work. If you can afford to pay somebody to do it, by all means do so. Other reasons you might pay someone is if you don't write well or you don't want to do it. It maybe worth outsourcing.

If you can't afford to pay someone to do it, just write, write, write as much as you can. Your writing will get better.

Blog several times a week. Whatever you decide to do as far as blogging is concerned, you want to make sure that you're consistent. If you only can do it once a week, make a commitment to do it once a week.

But if you can do it several times a week, it will be to your advantage to do so.

Tip 21

Dedicate time to becoming a subject matter expert. If you love what you do, or it's new for your but you love it and you're committed to it, you want to spend some time becoming a subject matter expert.

I advise listening to audio in your car. Zig Zigler said, "make your car an Automobile University." In other words, while you're in your car, listen to something on your area of expertise.

You can listen to a CD of an expert talking about your particular subject matter. You can also read books in your subject matter as well. I advise reading 1 hour a day in your area of expertise.

I do it first thing in the morning. I learn a lot of things that gives me ideas that I can blog about, that I can podcast about. This is a great thing to do.

Tip 22

Eliminate time wasters. This is something that is a struggle for me. I know it is for a lot of other business owners as well.

We get caught up in email and webinars that we're listening to for other people, surfing the internet, doing research.

Eliminate these time wasters and stay focused on what your high-value activities are. What things will add the most value for you?

Hopefully you have a goal you are working on, your one goal that you're working on that affects everything else that you do. Maybe it's revenue.

Then you have your goals or tasks- things that you have to do in order to accomplish your goal. Stay focused on that.

When you start your day, what's the most important thing that you need to work on? Then do that thing.

If there's something that you do not know how to do, just Google it. Don't get stuck on one thing. Chances are there is hundreds of thousands of websites on that one thing telling you how to do it. Also you can outsource it.

Tip 23

Dedicate time to working on your business, not just in your business every day. We get caught up in go go go go go. 12 hours, 16 hours every single day working in our business.

We have to take the time to work on our business, or else it would never run without us. Spend time working on your business. We talked about, just briefly, systems. Creating systems while you're working on your business is important.

Tip 24

Get a coach as soon as you can. Hire a coach. A coach will help you do things that you know you should do, but maybe you haven't.

You've been putting it off, putting it off, putting it off. A Coach will hold you accountable. There's all types of coaches for different things, different skills. There are Book coaches, Marketing coaches, Life coaches, Sales coaches and Business coaches just to name a few.

Tip 25

Your main job is to build relationships, especially through email marketing. You want to build relationships with your customers.

You want to give them good valuable content. Then you want to work towards building the relationship. Ask them questions. Create a survey through Survey Monkey. Post a survey on Facebook.

On social media, listen to the problems that people are complaining about or asking questions on. Offer products and services that solve those problems.

Before you try to sell, you want to try to build a relationship with those potential customers.

Tip 26

Join a mastermind group. This is very valuable, having like-minded individuals in a group with you that will help you take your business to the next level.

Basically you have 5 or 6 people who come together and during the hot seat you have an issue that you need help with and you will have 5 people who will help you come up with solutions to help you solve your problem, issue or challenge that you're facing.

It really opens your eyes up to things that you may have never considered before.

Tip 27

You will work and work and work, and then suddenly you'll see the fruits of your labor. What happens is the momentum starts to build and then it's like the snowball effect and then you start to see the fruits of your labor.

Tip 28

You should set daily goals and work on them every day. This will just give you an idea of where you are so you can check your progress. Take massive action. Don't just do one little thing and then one little thing tomorrow and then expect for things to change. If you want massive results, you've got to take massive action.

Tip 29

Learn about virality. I learned this from Sean Mize and I really started to read different books about this. This is important as far as making things stick, getting people to take action over all the noise that they hear and all the other businesses that are marketing to them.

Tip 30

Listen to podcasts in your area of expertise. Read books on your area of expertise, and if you don't have a lot of time, I like audio books, but I also like the books on Amazon Kindle as well.

Never stop learning. Even if you've been in business for a long time or you never want to stop learning because things are changing so quickly.

Tip 31

Nothing is free, so if you sign up for something online, a service that you need and it's free, it's not really free. You're going to pay in some way, whether it's quality, or the service. If you have questions, you can't get anybody to help you. Just be careful with it being free. I understand you're a new business, you don't have the money to pay, but nothing is free.

Free will cost you more in the long run in time and money.

Tip 32

Buy all of your competitor's products, and see how you can make them better. Are there gaps in their products? Are their different ways that it could be improved upon? You can learn a lot from your competitors. You can learn a lot of things that you don't know and get ideas from your competitors. You definitely want to buy your competitors products and see how they present their information.

Tip 33

Think on paper. I got this from Earl Nightingale and I think it's so important. Whenever you have an issue, a challenge, a problem, take out a piece of paper. Put at the top of the paper whatever the issue is, and then you just sit down and write down all the solutions you can think of on that paper. Just write and keep writing until you can't think of anything else, and then your solution will sometimes appear. Sometimes it takes a day or two.

Tip 34

Give before you expect to get. Most people think, "Okay, I'm going to get online, I'm going to sell my products, I'm going to be a millionaire." Well, it doesn't really work that way. You have to give before you expect to get anything. You will give a lot of content away. You'll have to touch potential customers or clients so many different times before they'll actually stand up and take notice, so you'll definitely have to give before you can expect to get anything.

Tip 35

Learn about list building. You'll hear it over and over again online, "The money is in the list." If you have a list, you could potentially have money in the bank if you will follow up and provide valuable content. Research indicates that each name on your list is worth $1 per month to you. I was just listening to someone last week saying that each name on his list was worth $100 to him. That's pretty good.

Tip 36

Learn as much as you can about finding or getting free traffic. When you start an online business, you become a Writer, a Marketer, Social Media Marketer, Search Engine Optimization expert, a Copywriter, a sales person, and on and on. You don't just take on whatever your business is. You take on all these other roles as well. Even if you can afford to hire someone to do all these positions, you still want to know how to do them so you have some way to check to make sure things are done correctly.

Tip 37

As far as your website, use a lot of white space on your website. Break things up, break up paragraphs. Use short sentences. Use a lot of graphics, and then make sure you save your graphics as a keyword (alt text), one of your keywords. Use short paragraphs.

Tip 38

Use several modalities when you're presenting information to your potential customers or your customers-Video, images, audio, or text. You want to use a combination of each.

Tip 39

Learn copywriting. The copywriting is how you present information or how you sell to your customer with text on your website. This could be web copy. This could be a sales page. You want to be able to persuade the customer to buy your products, and this type of writing is the way to do that.

Tip 40

It will never be perfect. Whatever you're trying to work on, or it will never be perfect. Just make it as good as it can be, and then improve it as you see fit. Don't get caught up in, "I'm still working on this, I'm still working on this," and then 3 months later you're still working on the same thing. Just make it as good as you can make it, and then go ahead and put it out or post it.

Improve as you go. Just do the best you can, get your stuff out there, get your website done, and then just improve as you go. Having an online business, it takes work, it takes time. Nothing happens overnight.

Tip 41

Understand your customers' pain points. You cannot sell anything to a customer if you don't know what their problems are, what their challenges are, what issues they're facing. You need to know what their pain points are. What issues are they dealing with? If you don't know, you need to conduct a survey. You can do it easily on Facebook, or Survey Monkey. People will be glad to tell you what they think. If you don't want to do that, or you don't get any responses, you can look at the forums in your niche. You can Google your "niche forums" and you will see all kinds of information about what problems people are having in your niche. You can also go to Yahoo Answers for information about what problems your niche is having. One thing you can do is you can look at the Amazon reviews for books that would be in your niche and see what people are looking for, what kind of information they're looking for. You can look at the groups on Facebook and LinkedIn, and sometimes you can get an indication of what people are looking for, what problems they're having, what questions they're asking.

Tip 42

Have a plan for your website. I am over the top all the time. I always have a vision for this big website, but you have to think of a website as an onion. It has layers. You really want to make sure that when you create a website that you create it with your sales funnel in mind, as well as the way you want your customer to come in to your website, or how they may come into your website, and how they're going to do what you want them to do in as few steps as possible. You want to really have a plan for your website, and if you don't understand this or need help with this, sometimes a web designer can really be beneficial in this. You want to see your website through the eyes of your potential customer.

Tip 43

Online everything revolves around keywords, so you want to know the keywords for your particular area of expertise. Google Keyword Planner is something that you can use to find out what keywords your customers are looking for. Also keywords will tend to be used as hashtags as well. Of course you can go to Amazon to see what books are the top, best sellers. That will give you an idea. Amazon has a tool implanted or embedded into their website that if you start typing something you'll see auto suggestions. Google and YouTube does this as well. This will give you an idea. The Google keyword tool is a little bit more comprehensive.

Every online business owner must know how to do SEO (search engine optimization). If you have a word press website, you need to have some basic word press skills, social media marketing skills, you need to have some writing skills because you have to put out a lot of content. You have to do videos for YouTube. You'll write content for your website. You have to write blog posts, post articles and post comments on different blogs. You have to do some writing.

Tip 44

You want to automate everything that you can. I use Hootsuite to automate my Social Media. I use Aweber as my Autoresponder to automate my email messages to my customers. I set my Wordpress to post my preloaded blog posts on certain days well in advance. I work with a VA for retweeting my blogposts.

Tip 45

Napoleon Hills quotes, "Your big opportunity may be right where you are now." Pay attention to all the unique opportunities around you.

Tip 46

Sometimes in online business you make your money on the back end, not necessarily on the front end. For example: you might have a joint venture with someone, and maybe you give them all the profits on the front end, or you only make 50% on the front end, and then you make the profits on the back end. Basically what that means is let's say for example that you do a joint venture with someone on a free webinar, and then you sell a boot camp at the end of the webinar, $997, and you have this Influencer in your niche that gets the $997 and then you have the customer for the duration, the lifetime of that customer. Let's say for example you have a $10,000 coaching program so you would make 100% of the profits of that on the back end. You will also make the profits on other products that you will sell to that customer. Just maybe on the front end you don't make any money. Sometimes you do, sometimes you don't. Maybe you have marketing expenses, but you're making money from the marketing but you're putting that money back into your business, so you're not necessarily profiting per se from that money, but the money on the back end, you will profit from that where you can actually use that money to pay salaries.

Tip 47

Avoid areas of business or online business that have no competition. It could be that there's no market for that business, or for that industry.

Tip 48

If you're going to be successful in an online business, you need to test and track everything. You want to know where customers are coming from or potential prospects are coming from. What page they're coming in, how long they're staying on your website, what they are buying, what they are not buying? You just want to know every step of the way what part of the processes need to be worked on. What gets measured gets managed.

Tip 49

There is power in taking action. Find what is unique, different, innovative, and create a business around that. Don't delay, do it now.

Tip 50

You want to really be authentic. Be vulnerable. Don't try to be something that you're not, don't try to do something just because someone else is. Or copy somebody else's business. You want to be true to who you are and what it is that you really want to do.

Tip 51

Finish what you start. Buy one program, finish it before starting on something else. This is something else as business owners we get caught up in the next shiny object, so we have a whole bunch of stuff going on at one time, and nothing's being finished, so you want to make sure that you're finishing the things that you're starting.

Tip 52

Let's talk about cost to start an online business. Even though starting an online business is low cost, there still are some costs. If you have a business online, you more than likely will have to have some type of website. With the website you have hosting which is a few dollars a month. Less than $10, usually if it's through Host gator or Blue gator. A domain I like is godaddy- less than $10 a year. You have to have some type of email management software- auto responder. This is one way if a customer signs up for something free on your website, they put in their email address. This is a way that you can capture that email and stat to build that relationship and sell to them. This could be $20 and up per month depending on who you choose. If you do webinars, and I do advise you to do webinars, if you're interested in having a sustainable business that grows that makes a pretty good amount of money on its own, the webinar system I use is Gotowebinar. I like Gotowebinar, but there's also Webinar Jam. Some people use Google hangout.

Tip 53

Use hashtags. Hashtags are your keywords that potential customers will use to find you. Hashtags got their start on Twitter. As most people would use the # sign with their keywords. Customers could then search those words with the hash sign in front of the keywords to find information they were looking for.

Tip 54

Become a content creating machine. Create YouTube videos-lots of them. Take content from an article, turn it into a video. Turn an article into a PowerPoint and then upload to Slide share.

Tip 55

In *The Laptop Millionaire* Mark Anastasi says the following:

Millionaire secret

Money is nothing but the measure of the value you create for other people

Millionaire secret money = Value X leverage

Millionaire secret Work for passive income, not earned income.

Millionaire secret sell products, don't sell your time

Millionaire secret. Get a mentor and copy a proven success formula. Instead of going for the trial and error approach, you include a successful business formula.

Tip 56

Automate all income streams as soon as possible. Automate the Upsell, Downsell and as much of your sales process as possible. Offer your products or services through some of your emails in your autoresponder. I usually try to sell something to my clients or customers every third or fourth email. Also offer your products or services next to your blog posts. Focus on Automating as much of your business as soon as possible. Always have an Upsell.

Tip 57

Become an affiliate if you want to make money sooner rather than later. Become an affiliate for products you use and believe in. Write an article on these products or services. You can write a review or write an article and mention the product or service and put a link in it for more information.

Tip 58

Keywords. Know your Keywords. Know what your customer's problems, issues, challenges. I can't say this enough. These would be the keywords. What questions might they be asking? Know your customer's language. Realize that the words you use might not be the same words your clients are using. Use Google Keyword planner for this. It's free.

Tip 59

Of course you'll need an internet connection. You'll have to spend money on education, you'll have to learn about SEO, social media marketing, internet marketing. You have to learn about copywriting. These books will cost money, so you have to add that in. If you're not good at copywriting, at least initially, you have to have some type of sales letter software, and then you have to have money for marketing. You have to have some way to get the word out. You can do a lot of things that are free, but you may want to spend money on marketing for Facebook ads. You have to have the money to do that. You have to figure that in at the beginning, that these things will cost money.

Tip 60

Decide what time of lifestyle you want and then create a business around that.

Tip 61

Focus on backend products not front end products. The money is in the backend. In other words, you might sell one product to start with, but the money is in the products you will sell month after month, year after year.

Tip 62

Don't put all your eggs in one basket. If one thing fails, you want to have something else.

Tip 63

Every business is a marketing business.

Every business is a relationship business. Build relationships with your customers. Communicate often with your customers.

Tip 64

Put money back into your business. Put some of the profits back into your business. Don't spend all of your profits. In order for your business to stay in business, it takes money.

Tip 65

When in doubt raise your prices. Most people under estimate the value of the products or services they offer.

Tip 66

Test everything. Identify which advertising channels provide the most bang for your buck by testing.

Tip 67

"Nobody makes it to the top without mentors and a powerful Master Mind team." Robert G. Allen

Tip 68

In Million Dollar Habits, Brian Tracy said Concentrate single mindedly on your most important task & stay with it until it is done.

The 80/20 rule seems to apply to the subject of constraints or limitations that are keeping you from achieving your goal are within yourself; not in the world around you. They are contained in your own attitudes, beliefs, fears, or lack of a particular skill or quality. Only 20 percent of your constraints are external to you or to your business.

Develop the habit of looking into yourself for the solutions to your problems. Ask this question, "What is it in me that is holding me back from achieving this goal?"

Tip 69

"People react to buying messages for one of two reasons—to get pleasure or to avoid pain." (*Celebrity brand you*)

Tip 70

Jim Rohn said "Don't start the day until you have it finished. Don't start the week until you have it finished. Don't start the month until you have it finished. Plan your day."

What Jim Rohn meant by this is always plan your day before it starts, plan your week before it starts. Plan your month before it starts. This is so important. As entrepreneurs sometimes we can get caught up doing busy work but not the most important things we should be doing.

Always have a plan. Work from a plan.

Tip 71

Know your weaknesses. Hire out your weaknesses. Trying to do everything yourself is a mistake.

Tip 72

Use images to draw people in. Use images in your blog post, on your website, sales letter etc., Check out http://www.morguefile.com, http://www.deviantart.com/, http://www.ibiblio.org/ for images.

Tip 73

"For one thing, there's an essential human factor in every business endeavor. It doesn't matter if you have a perfect product, production plan and marketing pitch; you'll still need the right people to lead and implement those plans."

Tip 74

People buy transformations and outcomes. How will your product or service change your customer's life?

Tip 75

Read the top 10 books in your niche. Read articles on the top 10 blogs in your niche. Listen to the top 10 podcasts in your niche. Read the top 10 forums in your niche. Use your customer's language in all of your material.

Tip 76

Any task that does not earn you your hourly rate (at a minimum) should be outsourced.

Tip 77

"If you are willing to do more than you are paid to do, eventually you will be paid to do more than you do."

Tip 78

On Your LinkedIn Profile, be sure you use your Main Keywords in Your Current Job Title, Past Job Titles, Summary, Headline, Skills & Expertise.

Conclusion

A few things to remember is be patient, be consistent, know your target market. You must want to learn because you're not going to know everything from the beginning.

Dedicate time to working on your business, not just in your business. Dedicate time to building your business. You don't need a lot of fans or customers to make a lot of money.

Always have a call to action telling people what you want them to do. Always make an offer, whether it's in your email marketing. You can also do it in a webinar, on a sales page, or your blog post. Always give people something of value.

Diversify. Having multiple streams of income is imperative. Take massive action on everything you know you can do. Make a list, create a plan, and then do it now.

Outsource as much as you can, and then take action. You won't be sorry. Learn all you can. There are so many different ways to do things.

The most important: never quit. It won't happen overnight, but it will happen if you don't give up. Just keep adding value and helping as many people as you can.

Develop a Plan. "If you are failing to plan, you are planning to fail." A plan is essential for growth. Start with a list of things you need to do to increase your sales. Add to it as you come across more things that need to be done. "Create a definite plan for carrying out your desire, and begin at once, whether you're ready or not, to put it into action." -- Napoleon Hill

Develop a roadmap. There are probably at least 10 things you've been meaning to do to grow your business and just haven't. Well now is the time. Write them down, along with everything else you have to do to accomplish your goals.

Don't limit yourself. You can accomplish twice as much as you are currently by prioritizing and doing what is important and delegating the rest.

Take the most important Goal and write it down. Create a plan to achieve it.

What strategies you will use to accomplish them?

I need your help. When you go to the next page, Kindle gives you an opportunity to share your thoughts and opinions through your Facebook and Twitter account. If you believe your friends and family will benefit from this book, please share your thoughts with them. You might change someone's life, and I would be eternally grateful to you.

If you feel strongly about the contributions this book made to your life, please take a few seconds to post a 5-star review on Amazon. Very few people ever leave 5-star review. So it is a big deal if you do. Writing a 5-star review is like tipping me $25. I really appreciate the gesture. I feel like a million bucks whenever I get a glowing review.

If you have any questions, you can reach me via Shondamiles@yahoo.com. I will try to respond to your questions as soon as possible. You can also connect with me on Facebook and Twitter.

www.shondamiles.com

Twitter: https://twitter.com/ShondaMilesINT/

Facebook: https://www.facebook.com/ShondaMilesInternational/

About the Author

Shonda Miles has been self-employed for 18 years. She has owned businesses ranging from an online retail store to a Training Company.

Shonda Miles is the CEO of Shonda Miles International, a company helping organizations and individuals improve performance and achieve their goals. Shonda Miles is here to help you achieve your full potential. Her purpose is to help millions of people achieve their goals and live their God given talent.

Shonda Miles is an Author, Entrepreneur, Speaker, Personal Development Trainer, Business Consultant and Business Coach. She loves reading Nonfiction books, writing business books and shopping. Personal Development is her mission. Shonda speaks, blogs and writes about a variety of personal development topics such as Time Management, Success, Goal Setting and having a Positive Attitude.

Shonda's goal is to help others achieve the level of success they desire.

Shonda Miles is a MBA Graduate. She has several successful businesses.

Shonda Miles can be reached at info@shondamiles.com or via her website at www.shondamiles.com.

www.ingramcontent.com/pod-product-compliance
Lightning Source LLC
Chambersburg PA
CBHW070337190526
45169CB00005B/1941

* 9 7 8 1 5 3 3 5 3 7 0 7 2 *